Easy Steps to Chinese for Kids

轻松学中文

少儿版

Textbook

英文版

Yamin Ma
Xinying Li

北京语言大学出版社
BEIJING LANGUAGE AND CULTURE
UNIVERSITY PRESS

图书在版编目（CIP）数据

轻松学中文：少儿版：英文版. 2b ／ 马亚敏，李欣颖编著.
—北京：北京语言大学出版社，2012.5（2015.10重印）
（轻松学中文）
ISBN 978-7-5619-3272-8

Ⅰ.①轻… Ⅱ.①马…②李… Ⅲ.①汉语-对外汉语教学
—教材 Ⅳ.①H195.4

中国版本图书馆CIP数据核字（2012）第074292号

书　　名	**轻松学中文（少儿版）英文版 课本 2b** QINGSONG XUE ZHONGWEN (SHAO'ER BAN) YINGWEN BAN KEBEN 2b
责任编辑	王亚莉　孙玉婷
美术策划	王　宇
封面设计	王　宇　王章定
版式设计	北京鑫联必升文化发展有限公司
责任印制	姜正周

出版发行	北京语言大学出版社
社　　址	北京市海淀区学院路15号　邮政编码：100083
网　　址	www.blcup.com
电　　话	编 辑 部 8610-82303647/3592/3395 国内发行 8610-82303650/3591/3648 海外发行 8610-82303365/3668/3080
网上订购	8610-82303908　service@blcup.net
印　　刷	北京联兴盛业印刷股份有限公司
经　　销	全国新华书店

版　　次	2012年5月第1版　2015年10月第5次印刷
开　　本	889mm×1194mm　1/16　印张：6.25
字　　数	34千字
书　　号	ISBN 978-7-5619-3272-8/H.12052 07800

©2012 北京语言大学出版社

Easy Steps to Chinese for Kids (Textbook) 2b
Yamin Ma, Xinying Li

Editors	Yali Wang, Yuting Sun
Art design	Arthur Y. Wang
Cover design	Arthur Y. Wang, Zhangding Wang
Graphic design	Beijing XinLianBiSheng Cultural Development Co., Ltd.

Published by

Beijing Language & Culture University Press
No.15 Xueyuan Road, Haidian District, Beijing, China 100083

Distributed by

Beijing Language & Culture University Press
No.15 Xueyuan Road, Haidian District, Beijing, China 100083

First published in May 2012
Printed in China
Copyright © 2012 Beijing Language & Culture University Press

Website: www.blcup.com

ACKNOWLEDGEMENTS

A number of people have helped us to put the books into publication. Particular thanks are owed to the following:

- 戚德祥先生、张健女士、苗强先生 who trusted our expertise in the field of Chinese language teaching and learning

- Editors 王亚莉女士、唐琪佳女士、黄英女士、孙玉婷女士 for their meticulous work

- Graphic designers 王章定先生、李越女士 for their artistic design for the cover and content

- Art consultant Arthur Y. Wang for his professional guidance and artists 陆颖女士、孙颉先生、陈丽女士、凌琳女士 for their artistic ability in beautiful illustration

- 刘倩女士、徐景瑄、左佳依、陈子珏、南珊 who helped with the sound recordings and 徐景瑄 for his proofreading work

- 刘慧 who helped with the song recordings

- Chinese teachers from the kindergarten section and Heads of the Chinese Department of Xavier School 李京燕女士、余莉莉女士 for their helpful advice and encouragement

- And finally, members of our families who have always given us generous support

INTRODUCTION

- The primary goal of this series *Easy Steps to Chinese for Kids* is to help total beginners, particularly children from a non-Chinese background, build a solid foundation for learning Chinese as a foreign language.
- The series is designed to emphasize the development of communication skills in listening and speaking. Recognizing and writing characters are also the focus of this series.
- This series employs the Communicative Approach, and also takes into account the unique characteristics of the children when they engage in language learning at an early age.
- Each lesson has a song using all the new words and sentences.
- Chinese culture is introduced in a fun way.
- This series consists of 8 colour books, which cover 4 levels. Each level has 2 colour books (a and b).
- Each textbook contains a CD of new words, texts, listening exercises, *pinyin* and songs, and is supplemented by a workbook, word cards, picture flashcards and a CD-ROM.

COURSE DESIGN

- **Character** writing is introduced in a step-by-step fashion, starting with strokes, radicals and simple characters.
- *Pinyin* is not formally introduced until Book 3a, as we believe that too-early exposure to *pinyin* may confuse children who are also learning to read and write in their mother tongue.
- **Language skills in listening and speaking** are the emphasis of this series, and the language materials are carefully selected and relevant to children of this age group.
- **Motor skills** will be developed through all kinds

简介

- 《轻松学中文》（少儿版）旨在帮助那些母语为非汉语的初学儿童奠定扎实的汉语学习基础。
- 本套教材的目标是通过强调在听、说能力方面的训练来培养语言交流技能。同时，识字和书写汉字也是这套系列教材的重点。
- 教材中采用了交际法，并在课程设计中考虑到儿童在这个特定的年龄段学外语的特点。
- 每课配有一首歌曲，用歌曲的形式把当课的生词和句子唱出来。
- 中国文化的介绍是通过趣味性的活动来实现的。
- 本套教材分为四级，每级分为a、b两本彩色课本，共8本。
- 每本课本后附有一张CD，录有生词、课文、听力练习、拼音和歌曲。课本还另配练习册、词语卡片、图卡和CD-ROM光盘。

课程设计

- 汉字书写先从笔画、偏旁部首和简单汉字着手。
- 拼音从3a才开始系统介绍，因为小朋友过早学拼音可能会影响他们母语的阅读和书写能力的培养。
- 听、说技能的培养是本套教材的重点，所选语料适合小朋友的年龄段及其兴趣爱好。
- 小朋友的手部握笔掌控能力的培养是通过各种精心设计的有趣的活动来实现的，这些活动可以是画线、画图、上色、描红、做手工等。
- 认知能力的培养是儿童早期教育的一个重点。

of fun and interesting activities, including drawing lines and pictures, colouring, tracing characters and making handicrafts, etc.

- **Cognitive ability** is a very important aspect of early schooling. By understanding the world around them through shapes, colours, directions, etc., children may find Chinese language learning more exciting, fun and relevant.

- **Logical thinking and imaginative skills** are nurtured through a variety of activities and practice, which create space for children to develop these skills as early as possible.

- **A variety of activities,** such as songs, games, handicrafts, etc., are carefully designed to motivate the children to learn.

- **Hands-on practice** is carefully designed throughout the series to make learning meaningful and enhance retention.

- **The pace** for developing language knowledge and skills takes a gradual approach, which makes it easy for children to build a solid foundation for learning Chinese.

通过图形、颜色、方向等的学习，小朋友认识了他们周边的世界，汉语学习也变得活泼、有趣，小朋友还能活学活用。

- 通过一系列精心设计的活动和练习，培养小朋友的逻辑思维和想象力。

- 各种各样、丰富多彩的活动，比如歌曲、游戏、手工等，都是为了激发小朋友学习汉语的积极性。

- 培养动手能力的练习贯穿始终，使小朋友学起来更有意思，也有助于他们掌握和巩固新学的内容。

- 学习的节奏由慢到快，循序渐进，使小朋友轻松打好汉语学习的基础。

COURSE LENGTH

课程进度

- This series is designed for young children or primary school students.

- With one lesson daily, primary school students can complete learning one level, i.e. two books, within an academic year.

- Once all the eight books have been completed, learners can move onto the series *Easy Steps to Chinese* (Books 1-8), which is designed for teenagers from a non-Chinese background.

- As this series is continuous and ongoing, each book can be taught within any time span according to the students' levels of Chinese proficiency.

- 本套教材专为幼儿或小学生编写。

- 如果每天都有汉语课，大部分学生可以在一年内学完一个级别的两本。

- 如果学完四级8本，学生可以继续学习同一系列的为非华裔中学生编写的《轻松学中文》（1—8册）。

- 由于本教材的内容是连贯的，教师可根据学生的水平来决定教学进度。

HOW TO USE THIS BOOK

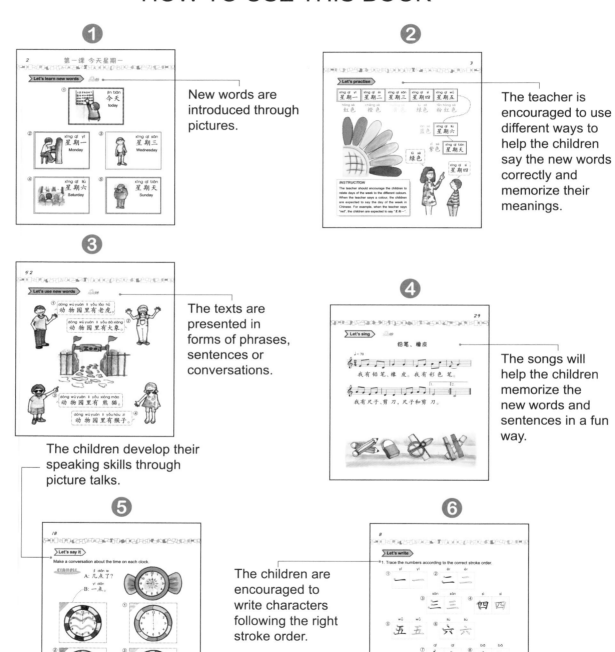

1 New words are introduced through pictures.

2 The teacher is encouraged to use different ways to help the children say the new words correctly and memorize their meanings.

3 The texts are presented in forms of phrases, sentences or conversations.

The children develop their speaking skills through picture talks.

4 The songs will help the children memorize the new words and sentences in a fun way.

5 The children are encouraged to write characters following the right stroke order.

6

⑦

Fun activities are designed to reinforce and consolidate language learning.

⑧

Such activities provide opportunities for the children to develop their logical thinking and imagination.

⑨

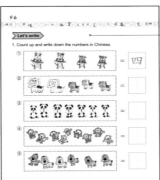

Such exercises are designed for the children to practise writing characters.

⑩

This section of Chinese culture can be introduced whenever the need arises.

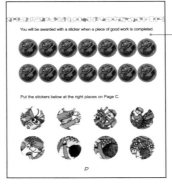

Stickers are given to the children when a piece of good work is completed.

CONTENTS 目 录

Let's learn new words 01

① jīn tiān
今天
today

② xīng qī yī
星期一
Monday

③ xīng qī sān
星期三
Wednesday

④ xīng qī liù
星期六
Saturday

⑤ xīng qī tiān
星期天
Sunday

Let's practise

xīng qī yī 星期一	xīng qī èr 星期二	xīng qī sān 星期三	xīng qī sì 星期四	xīng qī wǔ 星期五

hóng sè
红色

chéng sè
橙色

huáng sè
黄色

lǜ sè
绿色

fěn hóng sè
粉红色

lán sè
蓝色

xīng qī liù
星期六

zǐ sè
紫色

xīng qī tiān
星期天

lǜ sè
绿色

xīng qī sì
星期四

INSTRUCTION

The teacher should encourage the children to relate days of the week to the different colours. When the teacher says a colour, the children are expected to say the day of the week in Chinese. For example, when the teacher says "red", the children are expected to say "星期一".

4

Let's use new words

 02

jīn tiān xīng qī yī
今天 星期一。

①

jīn tiān xīng qī èr
今天 星期二。

②

jīn tiān xīng qī sān
今天 星期三。

③

My days of the week!

jīn tiān xīng qī sì
今天 星期四。

④

jīn tiān xīng qī tiān
今天 星期天。

⑦

jīn tiān xīng qī liù
今天 星期六。

⑥

jīn tiān xīng qī wǔ
今天 星期五。

⑤

Let's sing  03

一个星期有七天

week   day

♩= 70

一个星期有七天，有七天，有七天。星期一、

星期二、星期三、 星期四、星期五、

星期六， 今天 星期天！

Let's say it

Say the days of the week in Chinese.

One week during my winter holidays

①

jīn tiān xīng qī yī
今天 星期一。

②
jīn tiān xīng qī èr
今天 星期二。

③

jīn tiān xīng qī sān
今天 星期三。

④
jīn tiān xīng qī sì
今天 星期四。

⑤
jīn tiān xīng qī wǔ
今天 星期五。

⑥
jīn tiān xīng qī liù
今天 星期六。

⑦
jīn tiān xīng qī tiān
今天 星期天。

Let's write

1. Trace the numbers according to the correct stroke order.

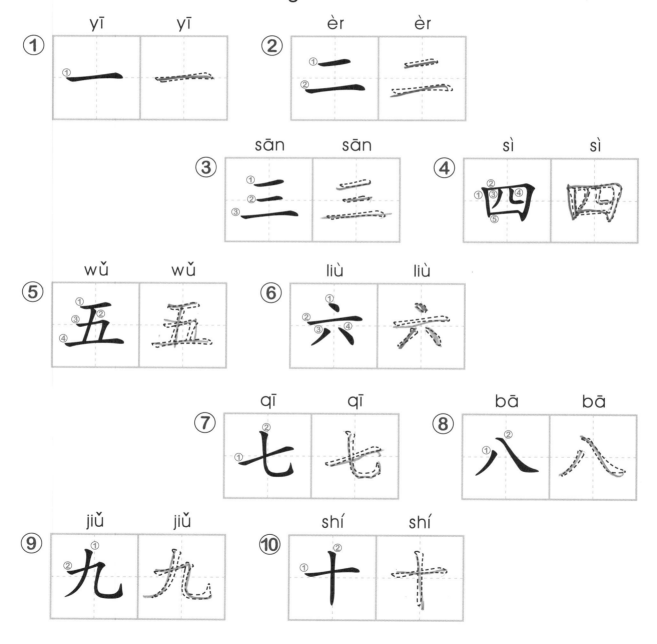

2. Add up the holes in the buttons and write down the sums in Chinese.

①  六

⑥ 二

② 九

⑦ 九

③ 五

⑧ 十

④ 十

⑨ 十

⑤ 四

⑩ 三

> **Let's play**

INSTRUCTION

When the teacher says an odd number, the children are expected to clap their hands. For example, when the teacher says "三", the children are expected to clap their hands once. When the teacher says an even number, the children are expected to stamp their feet. For example, when the teacher says "十二", the children are expected to stamp their feet once.

Some odd numbers:

yī	sān	wǔ	qī	jiǔ
一	三	五	七	九

shí yī	shí sān	shí wǔ	shí qī	shí jiǔ
十一	十三	十五	十七	十九

Some even numbers:

èr	sì	liù	bā	shí
二	四	六	八	十

shí èr	shí sì	shí liù	shí bā	èr shí
十二	十四	十六	十八	二十

> **Let's try it**

Trace the shapes with the colours given. Count up each shape and say the numbers in Chinese.

◯	△	⬡	⬭	☆	▢
31	6	1	8		4

It's time to work

Draw what you would like to do each day.

①

jīn tiān xīng qī yī
今天 星期一。

②

jīn tiān xīng qī èr
今天 星期二。

③

jīn tiān xīng qī sān
今天 星期三。

④

jīn tiān xīng qī sì
今天 星期四。

⑤
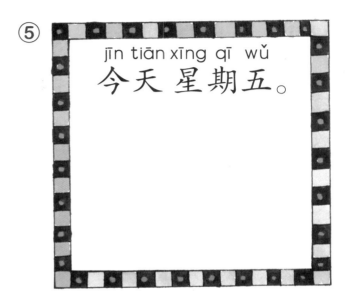

jīn tiān xīng qī wǔ
今天 星期五。

⑥

jīn tiān xīng qī liù
今天 星期六。

⑦
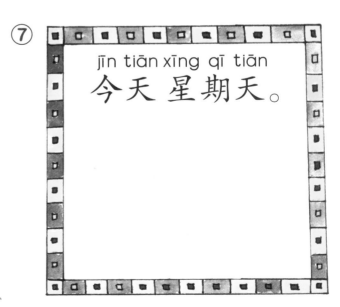

jīn tiān xīng qī tiān
今天 星期天。

第二课 几点了

① jǐ diǎn le
几点了
What time is it?

② yī diǎn
一点
1 o'clock

③ liǎng diǎn
两点
2 o'clock

④ bā diǎn
八点
8 o'clock

⑤ shí yī diǎn
十一点
11 o'clock

Let's practise

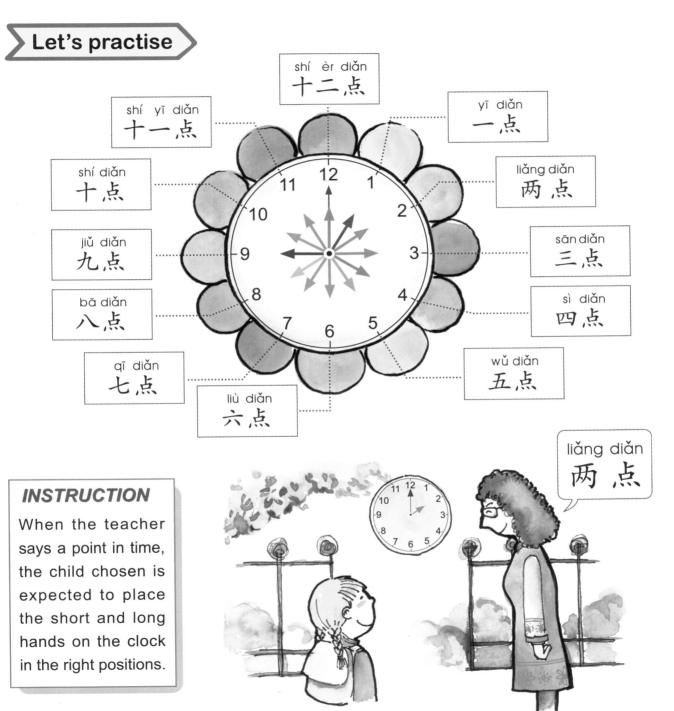

shí èr diǎn
十二点

shí yī diǎn
十一点

yī diǎn
一点

shí diǎn
十点

liǎng diǎn
两点

jiǔ diǎn
九点

sān diǎn
三点

bā diǎn
八点

sì diǎn
四点

qī diǎn
七点

wǔ diǎn
五点

liù diǎn
六点

liǎng diǎn
两点

INSTRUCTION

When the teacher says a point in time, the child chosen is expected to place the short and long hands on the clock in the right positions.

Let's use new words ◎05

jǐ diǎn le
几点了？

shí èr diǎn
十二点。

yī diǎn
一点。

shí yī diǎn
十一点。

liǎng diǎn
两点。

shí diǎn
十点。

sān diǎn
三点。

jiǔ diǎn
九点。

sì diǎn
四点。

bā diǎn
八点。

wǔ diǎn
五点。

qī diǎn
七点。

liù diǎn
六点。

> **Let's sing**  06

几点了

♩ = 70

一点、 两点、 三点、四 点，五点、

六点、 七点、八 点，九点、 十点、

十一点、十二点。 几点了？十 二 点。

Let's say it

Make a conversation about the time on each clock.

EXAMPLE

jǐ diǎn le
A: 几点了？

yī diǎn
B: 一点。

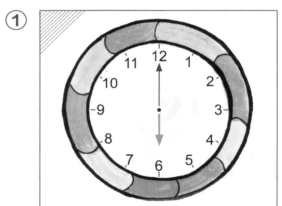

①

②

③

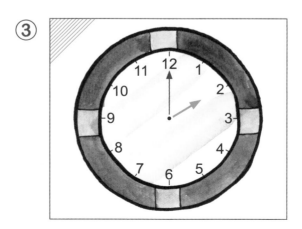

④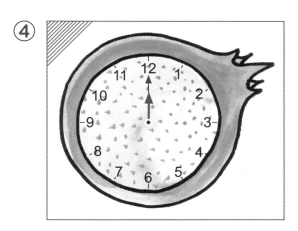

⑤

⑥

⑦

⑧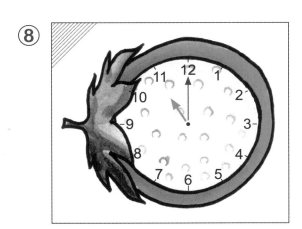

⑨

> **Let's write**

1. Write down the numbers in Chinese.

①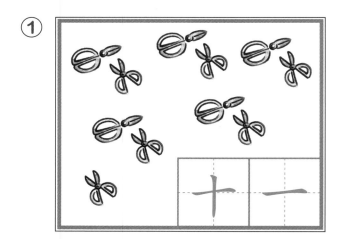

②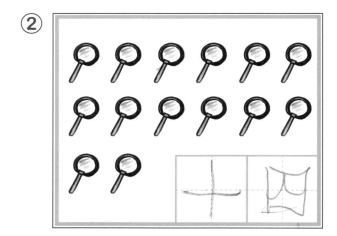

③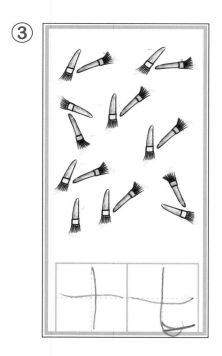

④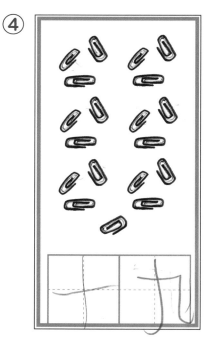

⑤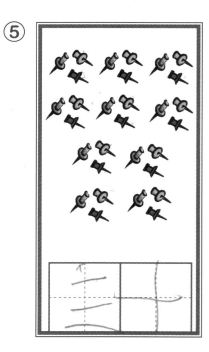

2. Draw three types of shapes and colour them in. Count up and write down the numbers in Chinese.

It's your turn!

> Let's play

jǐ diǎn le
几点了？

sān diǎn
三点。

INSTRUCTION

The children can work in pairs. One child places the short and long hands on the clock in the right positions, while the other child says the time in Chinese.

Some examples:

yī diǎn	liǎng diǎn	sān diǎn	sì diǎn
一点	两点	三点	四点

wǔ diǎn	liù diǎn	qī diǎn	bā diǎn
五点	六点	七点	八点

jiǔ diǎn	shí diǎn	shí yī diǎn	shí èr diǎn
九点	十点	十一点	十二点

Let's try it

Draw the short hand on each clock and tell the time in Chinese.

EXAMPLE

It is "十二点" now. What time will it be 3 hours later?

sān diǎn

三点。

①

What time will it
be 1 hour later?

②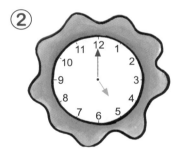

What time will it
be 3 hours later?

③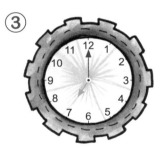

What time will it
be 2 hours later?

④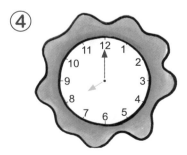

What time will it
be 3 hours later?

⑤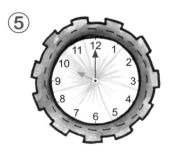

What time will it
be 2 hours later?

⑥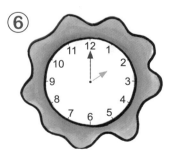

What time will it
be 3 hours later?

It's time to work

1. Say the time in Chinese and put the pictures in order.

①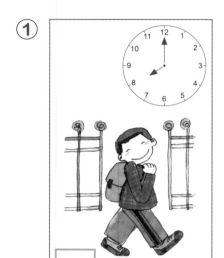

②

1

③

④

⑤

⑥

2. Write down the time in Chinese.

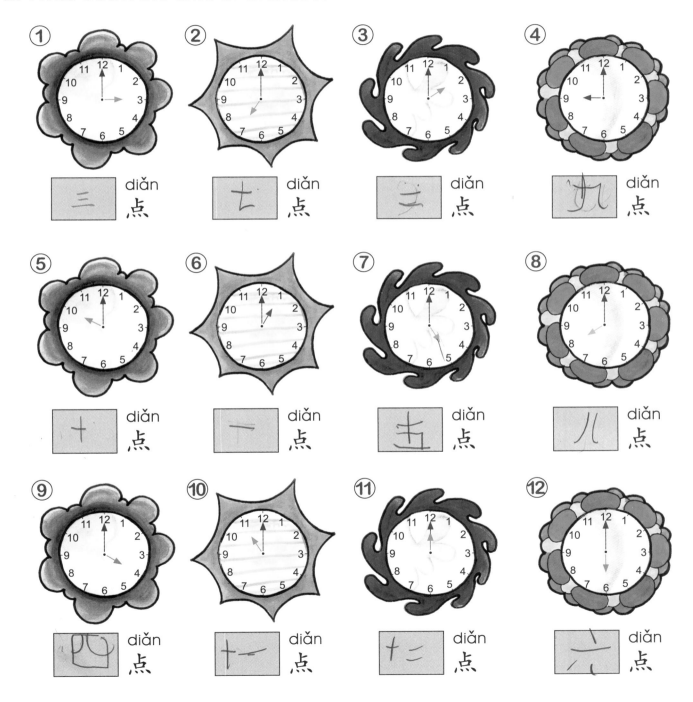

> **Let's learn new words** 07

①

qiān bǐ
铅笔
pencil

②
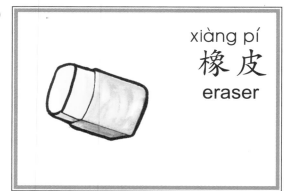

xiàng pí
橡皮
eraser

③
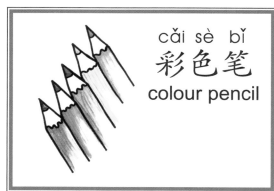

cǎi sè bǐ
彩色笔
colour pencil

④
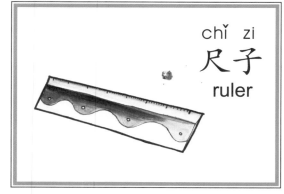

chǐ zi
尺子
ruler

⑤

jiǎn dāo
剪刀
scissors

Let's practise

Say one phrase for each picture.

qiān bǐ
铅笔

EXAMPLE

hóng sè de qiān bǐ
红色的铅笔

① chǐ zi
尺子

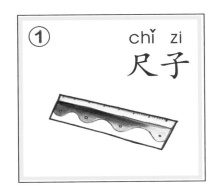

② jiǎn dāo
剪刀

③ xiàng pí
橡皮

④ shū zi
梳子

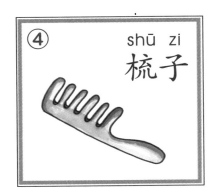

⑤ yá shuā
牙刷

⑥ xié zi
鞋(子)

⑦ yī fu
衣服

Let's use new words

①

wǒ yǒu qiān bǐ
我 有 铅笔。

②

wǒ yǒu xiàng pí
我 有 橡皮。

③

wǒ yǒu cǎi sè bǐ
我 有 彩色笔。

④

wǒ yǒu chǐ zi hé
我 有 尺子和
jiǎn dāo
剪刀。

Let's sing

铅笔、橡皮

我有铅笔、橡 皮。我有彩色 笔。

我有尺子、剪 刀，尺子和剪 刀。

Let's say it

Say one sentence about each person/animal in the picture.

京京

dīng yī yǒu jiǎn dāo
丁一有剪刀。

丁一

乐乐

田力

jīn yú huì kàn shū
1 金鱼会看书。

xiǎo māo yǒu shū zi
2 小猫有梳子。

xiǎo gǒu yǒu shū zi
3 小狗有梳子。

jīng jing yǒu qiān bǐ
4 京京有铅笔。

tián lì yǒu wū guī   wán
5 田力有乌龟、玩

jù huǒ chē hé cǎi sè bǐ
具火车和彩色笔。

lè le yǒu chǐ zi hé
6 乐乐有尺子和

xiàng pí
橡皮。

> **Let's write**

1. Write down the numbers in Chinese.

① 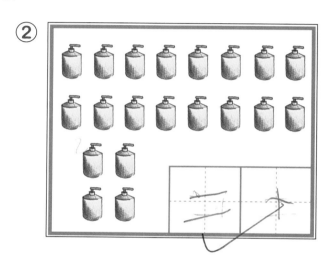 十 | 五

② 二十

③ 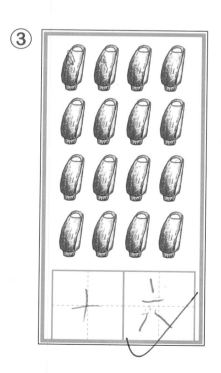 十六

④ 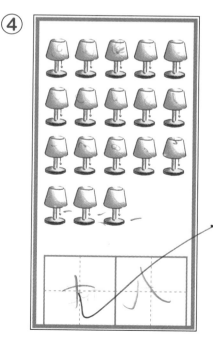 十八

⑤ 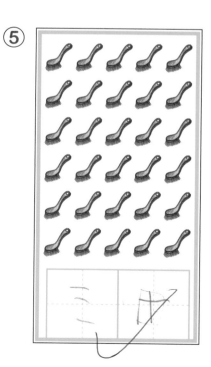 三十

2. Write down the missing numbers.

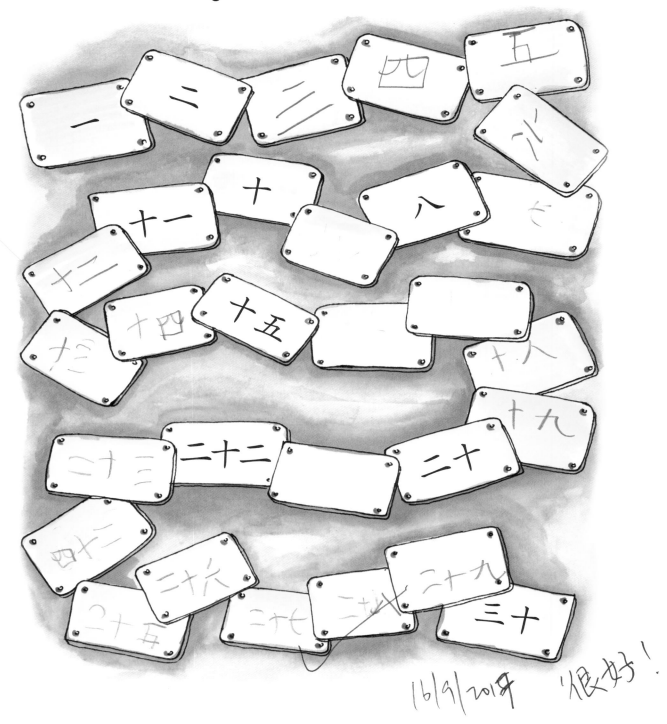

16/9/2019   很好！

Let's play

yì zhī qiān bǐ
一支铅笔

yì bǎ jiǎn dāo
一把剪刀

yí kuài xiàng pí
一块 橡皮

Some examples:

INSTRUCTION
When the teacher names an object, the children are expected to hold that object up. For example, when the teacher says "一支铅笔", the children are expected to hold up a pencil.

yì zhī qiān bǐ	liǎng zhī qiān bǐ	yí kuài xiàng pí
一支铅笔	两支铅笔	一块橡皮

sān kuài xiàng pí	yì bǎ chǐ zi	yì bǎ jiǎn dāo
三块橡皮	一把尺子	一把剪刀

yì zhī cǎi sè bǐ	wǔ zhī cǎi sè bǐ
一支彩色笔	五支彩色笔

Note: A measure word such as "支", "块", "把", is usually used and placed between a number and a noun in Chinese.

> **Let's try it**

Count up and write down the number of each item in Chinese.

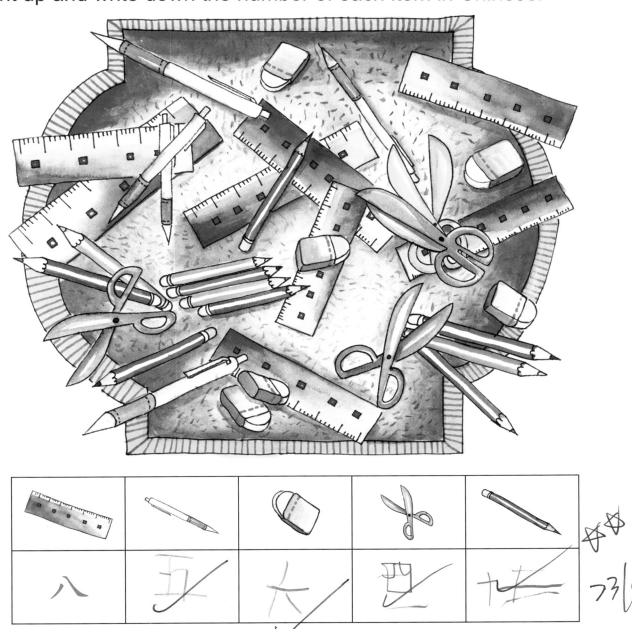

八	五	六	四	七

> **It's time to work**

Match the Chinese with the pictures and colour in the pictures.

① hóng sè de jiǎn dāo
红 色 的 剪 刀

② lán sè de xiàng pí
蓝 色 的 橡 皮

③ lǜ sè de chǐ zi
绿 色 的 尺 子

④ huáng sè de qiān bǐ
黄 色 的 铅 笔

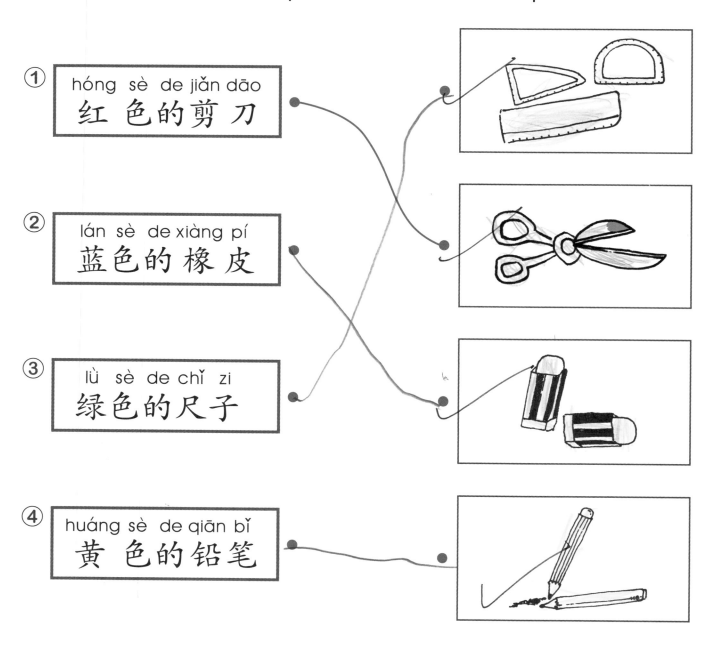

⑤
zǐ sè de yī fu
紫色的衣服

⑥
chéng sè de wán jù xióng
橙色的玩具熊

⑦
hēi sè de xié　zi
黑色的鞋（子）

⑧
fěn hóng sè de shū zi
粉红色的梳子

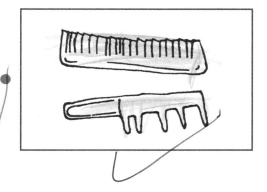

Let's learn new words

①

zhè
这
this

②

jiào shì
教室
classroom

③

zhuō zi
桌子
desk; table

④

yǐ zi
椅子
chair

⑤

shū
书
book

Let's practise

Say one sentence for each picture.

EXAMPLE

chǐ zi
尺子

zhè shì wǒ de chǐ zi
这是我的尺子。

① jiǎn dāo
剪刀

② xiàng pí
橡皮

③ cǎi sè bǐ
彩色笔

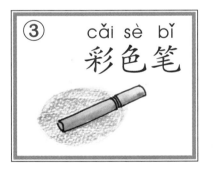

④ qiān bǐ
铅笔

⑤ jiào shì
教室

⑥ shū
书

⑦ zhuō zi
桌子

⑧ yǐ zi
椅子

Let's use new words

① zhè shì wǒ de jiào shì
这是我的教室。

③ zhè shì wǒ de shū
这是我的书。

② zhè shì wǒ de yǐ zi
这是我的椅子。

④ zhè shì wǒ de zhuō zi
这是我的桌子。

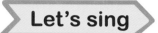 

我的教室

♩ = 70

这是我的 教室，我的 教室。 这是我的

1. 2.

桌子、椅子，这是我的 书。 书。

Let's say it

Describe the picture. Count up
the items. Say and write down
the numbers in Chinese.

zhè shì wǒ de jiǎn dāo
这是我的剪刀。

田力

丁一

乐乐

zhè shì wǒ de yǐ zi
这是我的椅子。

京京

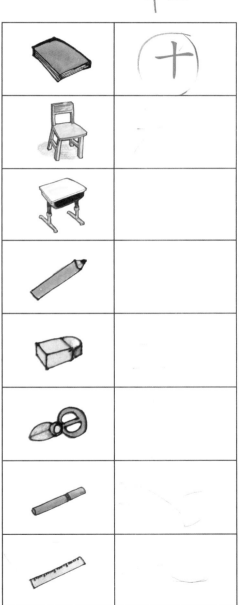

	十一
	十

> **Let's write**

1. Write down the numbers in Chinese.

①
三 十 五

②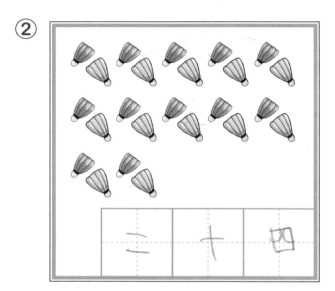
二 十 四

③
三 十 九

④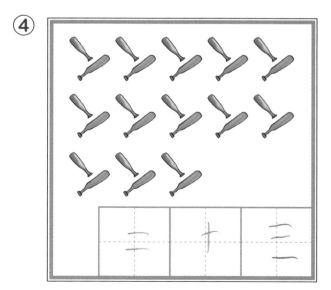
二 十 三

2. Write down the numbers in Chinese according to the patterns.

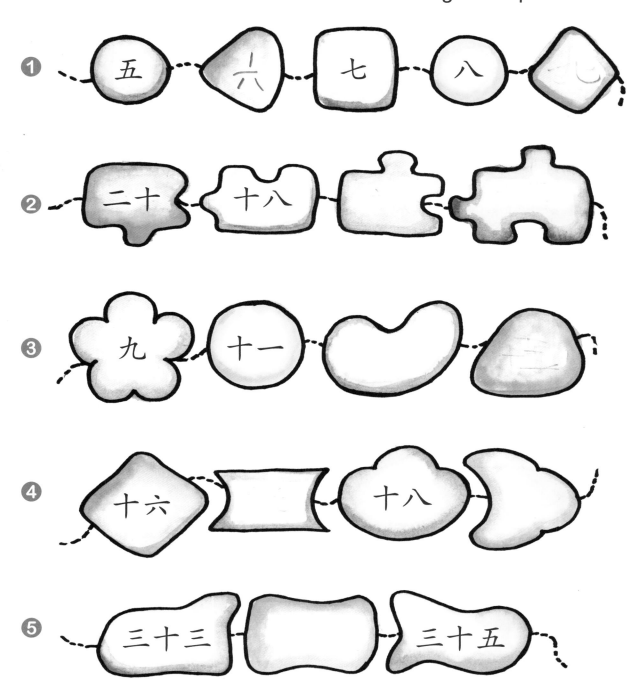

① 五　六　七　八

② 二十　十八

③ 九　十一

④ 十六　十八

⑤ 三十三　三十五

yì zhāng zhuō zi
一 张 桌子

yì bǎ yǐ zi
一把椅子

liǎng běn shū
两 本书

INSTRUCTION

When the teacher says a phrase, the children are expected to act accordingly. For example, when the teacher says "一张桌子", the children are expected to point to the desk, and when the teacher says "两支铅笔", the children are expected to hold up two pencils.

Some examples:

yì zhāng zhuō zi
一张桌子

yì bǎ yǐ zi
一把椅子

liǎng běn shū
两本书

sān zhī qiān bǐ
三支铅笔

sì kuài xiàng pí
四块橡皮

sān bǎ chǐ zi
三把尺子

yì bǎ jiǎn dāo
一把剪刀

liǎng zhī cǎi sè bǐ
两支彩色笔

Let's try it

Look around your school and your classroom. Count up each item listed below and fill in the boxes with the right numbers in Chinese.

1) There are ┃十二┃ jiān jiào shì 间教室 in my school.

2) There are ┃六┃ ge shū bāo 个书包 in my classroom.

3) There are ┃十九┃ zhāng zhuō zi 张 桌子 in my classroom.

4) There are ┃三十三┃ bǎ yǐ zi 把椅子 in my classroom.

5) There is/are ┃北┃ zhī qiān bǐ 支铅笔 in my pencil case.

6) There is/are ┃一┃ běn shū 本书 on my teacher's desk.

48

> **It's time to work**

1. Find their partners and write down the meaning of each phrase.

① zhuō
桌 ⬭ desk; table

zi
子

② jiào
教 ⬭

③ jiǎn
剪 ⬭

pí
皮

④ chǐ
尺 ⬭

bǐ
笔

⑤ yǐ
椅 ⬭

shì
室

⑥ xiàng
橡 ⬭

⑦ qiān
铅 ⬭

dāo
刀

2. Finish drawing the pictures and match them with the Chinese.

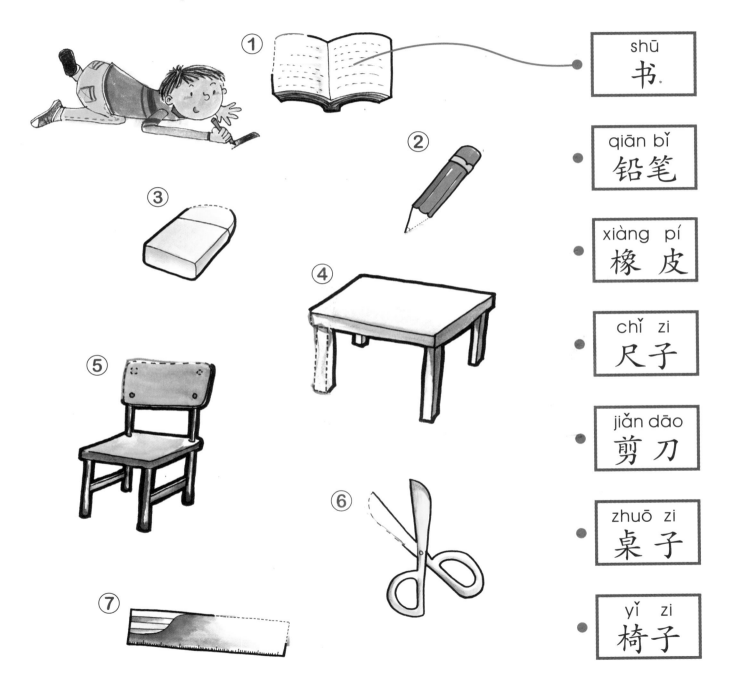

① shū 书

② qiān bǐ 铅笔

③ xiàng pí 橡皮

④ chǐ zi 尺子

⑤ jiǎn dāo 剪刀

⑥ zhuō zi 桌子

⑦ yǐ zi 椅子

Let's learn new words 13

①
dòng wù yuán
动 物 园
zoo

②
lǐ
里
inside

③
lǎo hǔ
老虎
tiger

④
dà xiàng
大 象
elephant

⑤
hóu zi
猴子
monkey

⑥
xióng māo
熊 猫
panda

5

> **Let's practise**

Circle the wrong part of the body of each animal and say it in Chinese.

gǒu
狗

EXAMPLE

gǒu de ěr duo
狗的耳朵

① māo
猫

② jīn yú
金鱼

③ wū guī
乌龟

④ dà xiàng
大象

⑤ lǎo hǔ
老虎

⑥ hóu zi
猴子

⑦ xióng māo
熊猫

HOMEWORK

Let's use new words

14

① dòng wù yuán li yǒu lǎo hǔ
动 物 园 里 有 老 虎。

② dòng wù yuán li yǒu dà xiàng
动 物 园 里 有 大 象。

③ dòng wù yuán li yǒu xióng māo
动 物 园 里 有 熊 猫。

④ dòng wù yuán li yǒu hóu zi
动 物 园 里 有 猴 子。

Let's sing 🎙️ 15

老虎、大象

动物 园里 有老虎、大象、猴子 和熊 猫。

动物园里 有老虎、大象、猴子 和熊猫。

Let's say it

Count up each animal.
Say and write down the
numbers in Chinese.

sì zhī gǒu
四只狗

	四只 zhī
	七只 zhī
	十二条 tiáo
	二头 tóu
	六只 zhī
	两只 zhī
	六只 zhī

> **Let's write**

1. Count up and write down the numbers in Chinese.

① = 四 √

② = 五 √

③ = 七 √

④ = 八 √

⑤ = 六 √

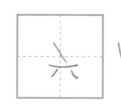

2. Add up and write down the sums in Chinese.

①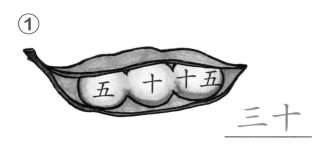

五 十 十五

三十

②

十 二十 七

_____

③

二 四 六

_____

④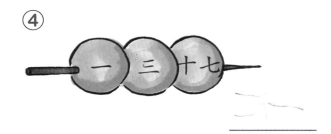

一 三 十七

_____

⑤

四 十四 二十

_____

⑥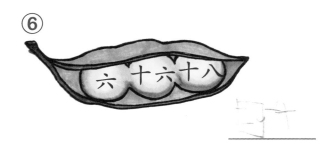

六 十六 十八

_____

⑦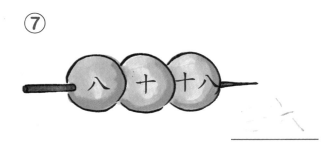

八 十 十八

_____

⑧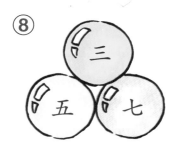

三 五 七

_____

Let's play

yì zhī lǎo hǔ　　liǎng zhī lǎo hǔ
一只老虎、两只老虎、
sān zhī lǎo hǔ　　jiā qi lai shì duō shao
三只老虎，加起来是多少？
　　　　　　　　add up　　how many

liù zhī lǎo hǔ
六只老虎。

INSTRUCTION

The children are asked to add up numbers and say the sums in Chinese as quickly as possible. For example, when the teacher says "一只老虎、两只老虎、三只老虎", the children are expected to say the sum "六只老虎" in Chinese.

Some examples:

yì zhī lǎo hǔ
一只老虎

yì zhī wū guī
一只乌龟

yì zhī hóu zi
一只猴子

yì zhī xióng māo
一只熊猫

yì zhī māo
一只猫

yì zhī gǒu
一只狗

yì tóu dà xiàng
一头大象

yì tiáo jīn yú
一条金鱼

Let's try it

Match the animal with the right tail.

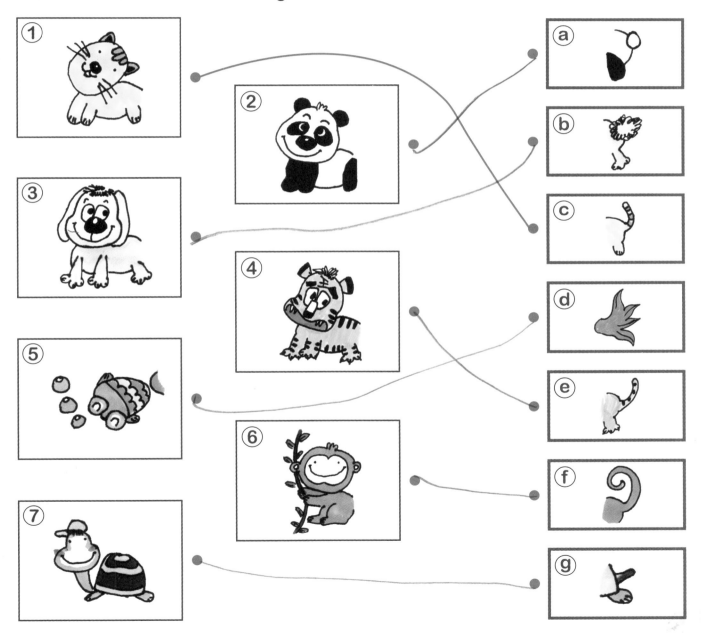

It's time to work

Find the animals in the picture. Count up and fill in the boxes with the right numbers in Chinese.

dòng wù yuán li yǒu
动 物 园 里 有：

✓ | 两 | zhī lǎo hǔ 只老虎

✓ | 七 | zhī hóu zi 只猴子

✓ | 三 | zhī xióng māo 只 熊 猫

| 五 | zhī gǒu 只狗

✓ | 六 | zhī wū guī 只乌龟

✓ | 二 | tóu dà xiàng 头大 象

✓ | 七 | tiáo jīn yú 条金鱼

> **Let's learn new words**

①
tù zi
兔子
rabbit

②
dà
大
big

xiǎo
小
small

③
duō
多
many

shǎo
少
few

Let's practise

Match the Chinese with the pictures.

① dà xiàng dà
大象大，
tù zi xiǎo
兔子小。

② hóu zi duō
猴子多，
lǎo hǔ shǎo
老虎少。

③ jīn yú duō
金鱼多，
wū guī shǎo
乌龟少。

④ xióng māo dà
熊猫大，
huáng gǒu xiǎo
黄狗小。

Let's use new words

① lǎo hǔ dà
老虎大。

② tù zi xiǎo
兔子小。

③ hóu zi duō
猴子多。

④ xióng māo shǎo
熊 猫 少。

Let's sing  ⊚18

大小、多少

♩ = 70

老虎、兔子,老虎、兔子,老虎大,兔子小。

猴 子、熊 猫,猴 子、熊 猫,猴 子 多,

1. 熊猫少。
2. 熊猫少。

> **Let's say it**

Say one sentence for each picture.

EXAMPLE

lǎo hǔ dà   tù zi xiǎo
老虎大，兔子小。

①

②

③

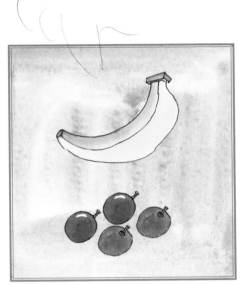

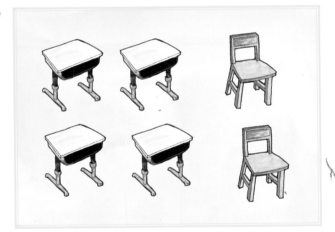

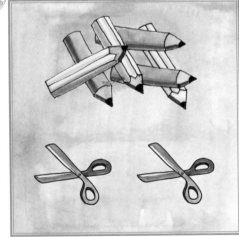

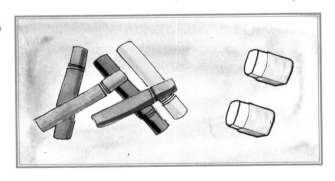

Let's write

1. Count up and write down the numbers in Chinese. Then match the animals with the food they eat.

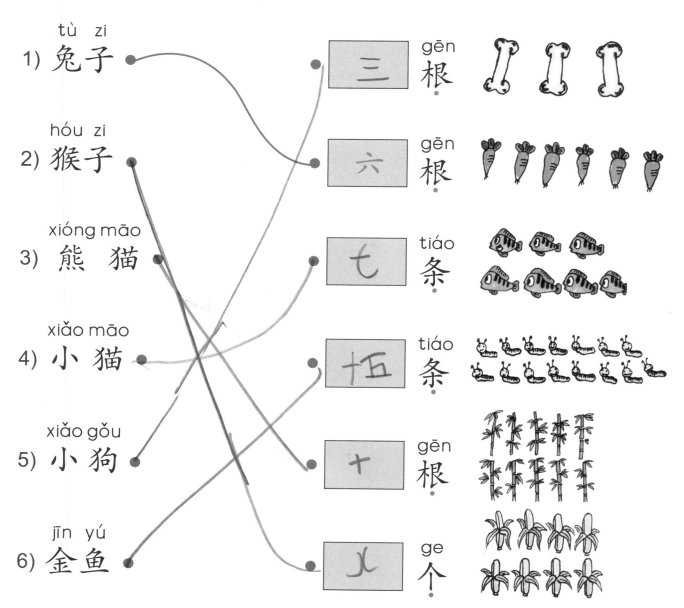

tù zi
1) 兔子

gēn
三 根

hóu zi
2) 猴子

gēn
六 根

xióng māo
3) 熊 猫

tiáo
七 条

xiǎo māo
4) 小 猫

tiáo
十五 条

xiǎo gǒu
5) 小 狗

gēn
十 根

jīn yú
6) 金鱼

ge
X 个

2. Count up each shape and write down the numbers in Chinese.

○	十六

⬭	十二

△	三十三

25/11/2017

□	八

Let's play

wǔ zhī lǎo hǔ　　sān zhī hóu zi
五只老虎，三只猴子。

lǎo hǔ duō　　hóu zi shǎo
老虎多，猴子少。

INSTRUCTION

The children are expected to compare and judge when doing this activity. For example, when the teacher says "五只老虎，三只猴子", the children are expected to say "老虎多，猴子少".

Some examples:

wǔ zhī hóu zi	sì zhī xióng māo	bā zhī māo
五只猴子	四只熊猫	八只猫

jiǔ zhī gǒu	liù zhī wū guī	shí tóu dà xiàng
九只狗	六只乌龟	十头大象

qī tiáo jīn yú
七条金鱼

Let's try it

Match the animals with the food they eat. Colour in the animals.

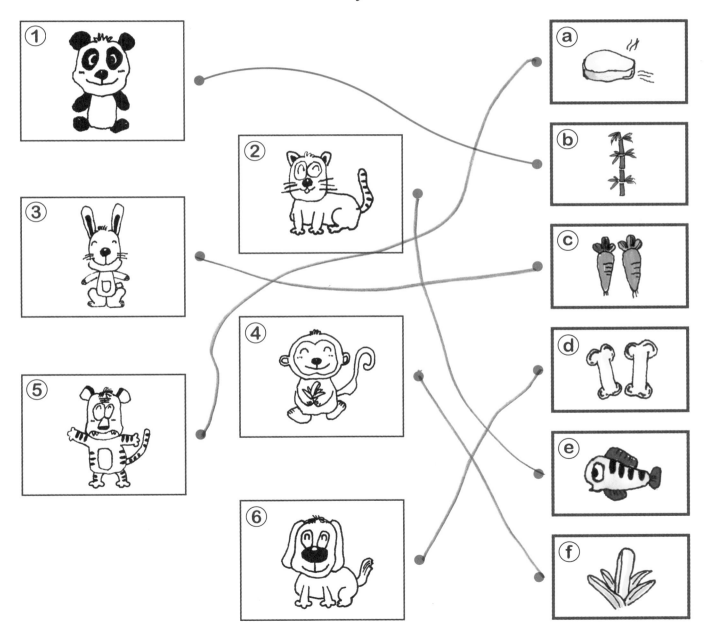

Describe the picture using the sentences given.

dà xiàng xǐ huan kàn shū
① 大象喜欢看书。

lǎo hǔ ài huà huàr
② 老虎爱画画儿。

wū guī měi tiān xiě zì
③ 乌龟每天写字。

dà xiàng yǒu wá wa
④ 大象有娃娃。

hóu zi ài chī xiāng jiāo
⑤ 猴子爱吃香蕉。

tù zi huì shuā yá
⑥ 兔子会刷牙。

xiǎo gǒu huì shū tóu
⑦ 小狗会梳头。

xiǎo māo huì chuān wà zi
⑧ 小猫会穿袜子。

Let's learn new words

① táng guǒ
糖果
candy

② dàn gāo
蛋糕
cake

③ bīng qí lín
冰淇淋
ice cream

④ qiǎo kè lì
巧克力
chocolate

Let's practise

Say which animal you like and which food you like eating.

nǐ xǐ huan shén me dòng wù?
你喜欢 什么 动物?

nǐ xǐ huan chī shén me?
你喜欢吃什么?

wǒ xǐ huan chī táng guǒ
我喜欢吃 糖果。

wǒ xǐ huan gǒu
我喜欢狗。

Some examples:

táng guǒ	dàn gāo	bīng qí lín	qiǎo kè lì	māo	gǒu
糖果	蛋糕	冰淇淋	巧克力	猫	狗

lǎo hǔ	hóu zi	dà xiàng	xióng māo	tù zi	jīn yú
老虎	猴子	大象	熊猫	兔子	金鱼

wū guī	cǎo méi	píng guǒ	xiāng jiāo	pú tao
乌龟	草莓	苹果	香蕉	葡萄

①

wǒ xǐ huan chī táng guǒ
我喜欢吃糖果。

wǒ xǐ huan chī dàn gāo
我喜欢吃蛋糕。

②

③

wǒ ài chī bīng qí lín
我爱吃冰淇淋。

wǒ ài chī qiǎo kè lì
我爱吃巧克力。

④

Let's sing ⦾21

糖果、蛋糕

我 喜欢吃　糖　果。我 喜欢吃　蛋　糕。

冰淇　淋、冰淇淋我爱　吃。巧克　力、巧克　力

我　爱　吃。　　我　爱　吃。

Let's say it

Count up each type of food. Say and write down the numbers in Chinese.

🍬	八
🍰	
🍨	
🍫	
🍎	
🍌	
🍒	
🍓	

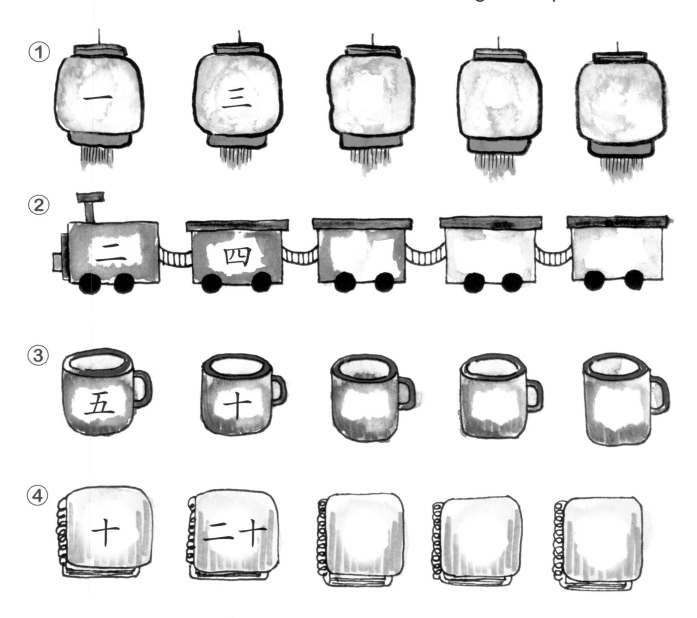

> **Let's write**

1. Write down the numbers in Chinese according to the patterns.

2. Fill in the boxes with the numbers in Chinese. Match the days of the week in Chinese with their meanings.

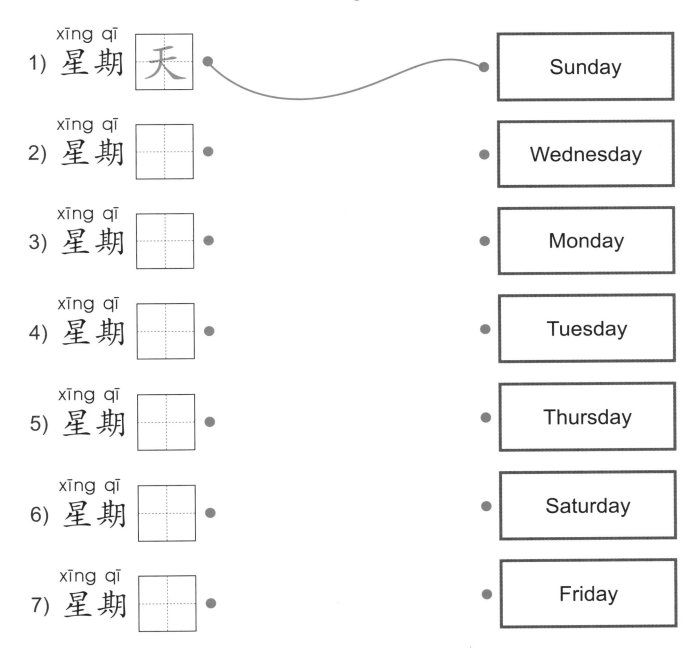

xīng qī
1) 星期 天 ●————————● Sunday

xīng qī
2) 星期 ☐ ● ● Wednesday

xīng qī
3) 星期 ☐ ● ● Monday

xīng qī
4) 星期 ☐ ● ● Tuesday

xīng qī
5) 星期 ☐ ● ● Thursday

xīng qī
6) 星期 ☐ ● ● Saturday

xīng qī
7) 星期 ☐ ● ● Friday

Let's play

píng guǒ
苹果

cǎo méi
草莓

xiāng jiāo
香蕉

Some examples:

① xiāng jiāo píng guǒ
香蕉、苹果……

② táng guǒ dàn gāo
糖果、蛋糕……

③ lǎo hǔ hóu zi
老虎、猴子……

④ qiān bǐ xiàng pí
铅笔、橡皮……

⑤ jiào shì zhuō zi
教室、桌子……

⑥ dà xiǎo
大、小……

⑦ bà ba mā ma
爸爸、妈妈……

⑧ xīng qī yī xīng qī èr
星期一、星期二……

Let's try it

Find the route for each person.

 我喜欢吃糖果。 我喜欢吃蛋糕。 我爱吃冰淇淋。  我爱吃巧克力。

六	二	十三	二十一	十七	十六	十二	十	一	十七	十四	十七	一
十四	四	六	二十	一	十五	一	二十三	三	二十四	十	二十	二
二十四	十二	八	四	十三	十四	二十一	七	五	二	十四	四	三
十一	九	十	十一	十二	二	十一	九	八	七	六	五	十三
一	八	十二	十四	十六	六	十三	十	十一	二	十一	十七	二
十三	七	六	十一	十八	一	十五	七	十二	十三	十四	一	七
三	四	五	十三	二十	二十二	十七	十九	六	一	十五	五	二十三
二	二十	二	九	十五	二十四	四	二十一	二十三	十二	十六	二十一	八
一	十	二十四	十一	十七	二十六	八	十四	二十五	三	十七	五	十四

> **It's time to work**

Describe the picture using the sentences given.

jīng jing xǐ huan chī táng guǒ
① 京京喜欢吃糖果。

lè le ài chī qiǎo kè lì
② 乐乐爱吃巧克力。

tián lì xǐ huan chī dàn gāo
③ 田力喜欢吃蛋糕。

dīng yī ài chī bīng qí lín
④ 丁一爱吃冰淇淋。

hóu zi ài chī xiāng jiāo
⑤ 猴子爱吃香蕉。

xióng māo huì chuān yī fu
⑥ 熊猫会穿衣服。

dà xiàng xǐ huan xiě zì
⑦ 大象喜欢写字。

lǎo hǔ yǒu qiān bǐ hé xiàng pí
⑧ 老虎有铅笔和橡皮。

中国文化 Chinese Culture

duān wǔ jié
端午节

lóng zhōu jié
（龙舟节）

Dragon Boat Festival

Dragon Boat Festival is celebrated on the fifth day of the fifth lunar month. Chinese New Year and Mid-Autumn Festival, together with Dragon Boat Festival, form the three major Chinese traditional festivals. Dragon Boat Festival is highlighted by dragon boat races, in which competing teams row their boats forward to the rhythm of pounding drums. The most popular food eaten on Dragon Boat Festival is "zongzi (粽子)". It was originally made and eaten in memory of the patriotic poet Qu Yuan (屈原). However, it has gradually evolved into a snack eaten during normal occasions as well.

A

1. Learn to make a paper boat.

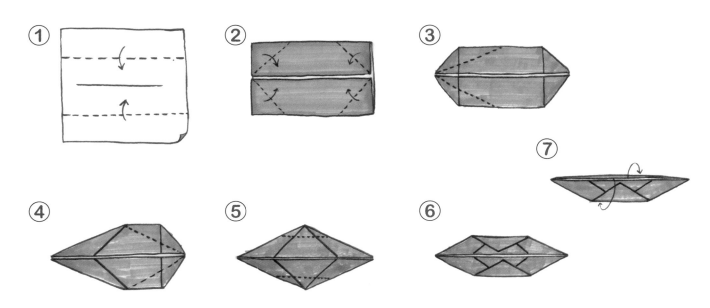

2. Colour in the dragon boat.

B

Find the stickers on Page D and put them at the right places.

duān wǔ jié   lóng zhōu jié
端午节（龙舟节）Dragon Boat Festival

词汇表 VOCABULARY

Lesson 1

今天	jīntiān	today
星期一	xīngqīyī	Monday
星期二	xīngqī'èr	Tuesday
星期三	xīngqīsān	Wednesday
星期四	xīngqīsì	Thursday
星期五	xīngqīwǔ	Friday
星期六	xīngqīliù	Saturday
星期天	xīngqītiān	Sunday
○ 星期	xīngqī	week
○ 天	tiān	day

Lesson 2

几点了	jǐ diǎn le	What time is it?
一点	yī diǎn	1 o'clock
两点	liǎng diǎn	2 o'clock
三点	sān diǎn	3 o'clock
四点	sì diǎn	4 o'clock
五点	wǔ diǎn	5 o'clock
六点	liù diǎn	6 o'clock

七点	qī diǎn	7 o'clock
八点	bā diǎn	8 o'clock
九点	jiǔ diǎn	9 o'clock
十点	shí diǎn	10 o'clock
十一点	shíyī diǎn	11 o'clock
十二点	shí'èr diǎn	12 o'clock

Lesson 3

铅笔	qiānbǐ	pencil
橡皮	xiàngpí	eraser
彩色笔	cǎisèbǐ	colour pencil
尺子	chǐzi	ruler
剪刀	jiǎndāo	scissors
○ 支	zhī	a measure word
○ 把	bǎ	a measure word
○ 块	kuài	a measure word

Lesson 4

这	zhè	this
教室	jiàoshì	classroom

桌子	zhuōzi	desk; table
椅子	yǐzi	chair
书	shū	book
○ 张	zhāng	*a measure word*
○ 本	běn	*a measure word*
○ 间	jiān	*a measure word*
○ 个	gè	*a measure word*

Lesson 5

动物园	dòngwùyuán	zoo
里	lǐ	inside
老虎	lǎohǔ	tiger
大象	dàxiàng	elephant
猴子	hóuzi	monkey
熊猫	xióngmāo	panda
○ 只	zhī	*a measure word*
○ 条	tiáo	*a measure word*
○ 头	tóu	*a measure word*

○ 加起来	jiā qilai	add up
○ 多少	duōshao	how many

Lesson 6

兔子	tùzi	rabbit
大	dà	big
小	xiǎo	small
多	duō	many
少	shǎo	few
○ 根	gēn	*a measure word*

Lesson 7

糖果	tángguǒ	candy
蛋糕	dàngāo	cake
冰淇淋	bīngqílín	ice cream
巧克力	qiǎokèlì	chocolate